Flemish Giant Rabbits

A Complete Flemish Giant Rabbits Pet Guide

Flemish Giant Rabbit Breeding, Buying, Care, Cost, Keeping, Health, Supplies, Food, Rescue and More Included!

By Lolly Brown

Foreword

Flemish Giant rabbit breeds are considered as the 'King of Rabbits' because of their huge size, personality and longevity. These breeds had been around since the 16th century, around 1860's in Belgium. The Flemish Giant's ancestors are Patagonian rabbits which are also large breeds. They have a reputation of being docile, playful and sweet.

Although Flemish Giant rabbits are truly a great choice as pets, these rabbits doesn't come with a thin instruction manual, but fear not! In this book you'll be easily guided on understanding your Flemish Giant rabbit, their behaviors, their characteristics, how you should feed and care for them and a whole lot more.

Embark on a wonderful journey of sharing your life with a Flemish Giant rabbit. Learn to maximize the great privilege of living with one and be able to share this unique and unforgettable experience just like many pet owners that came before you!

Table of Contents

Introduction

Flemish Giant Rabbits are known as 'Gentle Giants' in the rabbit world, they are also known as King of Rabbits because of their large size, great personality and long life. These breed was developed in Belgium around the 16th century. It is considered as 'Universal Rabbit' for its variety of purposes; it can be your pet, they are eligible for show and were originally bred for meat and fur animal. These rabbit breed have docile and gentle personalities. But what is it that makes these rabbits so popular?

There is no short answer to this question because, with Flemish Giant rabbits, there is just so much to love.

Introduction

The Flemish Giant rabbit is more than just a pet; it is a friendly, active and a loving companion. These rabbits are trainable, cuddly and energetic, plus they are very great family pets, although they may not be ideal for very young children. If you are thinking about adopting a rabbit or purchasing a doe or buck, the Flemish Giant rabbit is definitely a great breed to consider.

Before you bring a Flemish Giant rabbit home, however, you should be a responsible rabbit owner and learn everything you can about this breed and how to care for it properly.

Fortunately, this ultimate guide will teach you on how to be the best Flemish Giant rabbit owner you can be! Inside this book, you will find tons of helpful information about Flemish Giant rabbit; how they live, how to deal with them and realize the great benefits of owning one!

This book includes information about creating the ideal habitat and diet for your rabbit as well as tips for breeding and showing your Flemish Giant rabbit. You will also find in-depth health information for the breed including common health problems affecting it and the treatment options available.

The fluffy world of Flemish Giant rabbit breed awaits! What are you waiting for? Keep reading!

Glossary of Rabbit Terms

Agouti – A type of coloring in which the hair shaft has three or more bands of color with a definite break between.

Albino – A pink-eyed, white-furred rabbit.

ARBA – The American Rabbit Breeders Association; an organization which promotes rabbits in the United States.

Awn – The strong, straight guard hairs protruding above the undercoat in angora breeds.

Balance – An orderly and pleasing arrangement of physical characteristics promoting a harmonious appearance.

Bangs – Longer fur appearing at the front base of the ears and on top of the head in some woolen breeds.

Base Color – The color of the fur next to the skin.

Bell Ears – Ears that have large tips with distinct Flemish Giant or fall.

Belt – The line where the colored portion of the coat meets the white portion, just behind the shoulders.

Blaze – A white marking found on the head of the Dutch rabbit; the shape is wedge-like.

Bonding – A term used to describe two rabbits that have paired up together.

BRC – The British Rabbit Council, formed from the British Rabbit Society and the National Rabbit Council of Great Britain in 1934.

Broken Coat – A coat with guard hairs missing or broken in places, exposing the undercoat

Buck – An unaltered or intact male rabbit.

Buff – A rich, golden-orange color.

Caecotroph – Pellets of semi-digested food eaten from the anus for nutrition reasons.

Chinning – Rubbing the chin on objects of people to spread scent from glands under the chin.

Cobby – A term meaning stout or stocky in body; short legs.

Condition – The overall physical state of a rabbit in terms of its fur, health, cleanliness, and grooming.

Crossbreeding – Mating two different breeds.

Cull – The process of selecting the best rabbits from a litter and selling or slaughtering the rest.

Dam – A female rabbit that has produced offspring.

Doe – An unaltered female rabbit.

Flat Coat – Fur lying too close to the body, lacking spring and body as noted by touch.

FFlemish Giantping – A sign of happiness or contentedness; the rabbit fFlemish Giants over on his side and exposes his belly.

Fryer – A young meat rabbit no more than 10 weeks of age and weighing less than 5 pounds.

Gestation – The period of time between breeding and birthing (or kindling).

Guard Hair – The long, coarser hairs in a rabbit's coat which protect the undercoat.

Herd – A group of rabbits.

Inbreeding – Breeding of closely related stock.

Junior – A class of rabbits referring to those under 6 months of age.

Kindling – The process of giving birth to baby rabbits (kits).

Kindling Box – A box provided for a pregnant rabbit so she can make a nest and give birth.

Kit – A baby rabbit.

Line Breeding – A breeding program in which rabbits that are descended from the same animal are bred.

Litter – A group of young rabbits born to one doe at the same time.

Loose Coat – A condition of fur lacking density in the undercoat, often coupled with fine guard hairs resulting in a lack of texture.

Malocclusion – A misalignment of the rabbit's teeth.

Molt – The process of shedding or changing the fur, happens twice each year.

Nest Box – A box provided for a pregnant rabbit so she can make a nest and give birth.

Nursing – The process of kits suckling milk from the dam's teats; usually occurs twice a day.

Peanut – A rabbit with two dwarf genes; usually fatal.

Pelage – The fur coat or covering in a rabbit.

Pellets – May refer either to the rabbit's poop or its food.

Quick – The pink part of the nails/claws that contains the blood vessels and nerves.

Racy – Referring to a slim, slender body and legs.

Saddle – The rounded portion of the back between the rabbit's shoulder and loin.

 Self-Colored – A fur pattern where the hair colors are the same all over the body.

Sire – A male rabbit that has produced offspring.

Thumping – The practice of banging or stomping the hind legs on the ground to make a loud, thudding noise.

Ticking - A wavy distribution of longer guard hairs throughout the rabbit's coat.

Weaning – The process in which baby rabbits become independent of their dam, transitioning to solid food.

Wool – A term used to describe the fur of Angora rabbits.

Chapter One: Flemish Giant Rabbit in Focus

Flemish Giant rabbits may often time look like your protective brother, your supportive parents, your calm pal, your playful sibling or that very adorable kid you always wanted. In whatever attitude or mood it appeals, you can expect it to be docile yet interactive and a caring devoted pet you've always dreamed of.

The Flemish Giant rabbit is a breed of rabbit that is eligible for shows. They are irresistibly cute but it may not be the right choice for everyone. Before you decide whether or not it might be the right pet for you and your family, you need to learn and invest a significant amount of time in getting to know these animals.

In this chapter you will receive an introduction to the Flemish Giant rabbit breed including some basic facts and information as well as the history of how it came about. This information, in combination with the practical information about keeping Flemish Giant rabbit in the next chapter, will help you decide if this is the perfect rabbit companion for you.

Facts about Flemish Giant Rabbits

In this section you'll find some interesting fun facts about Flemish Giant rabbits, how to differentiate them through their body type, the types of their mane and history.

Flemish Giant rabbits are large sized rabbits that have a large semi-arch type body and a broad head with erect ears. They like to be around people and have a knack for a good time but don't let their cuteness fool you, like any rabbits, they can get scared and be wary especially around strangers, and if it feels threatened it may cause aggression, which is why it is advisable that owners should socialize them at an early age.

Male Flemish Giant rabbits have broader heads than females. The females have dewlap or a large flap of skin under their chins to protect and keep their baby bunnies warm. There are seven official colors for the Flemish Giant breed these are Black, Blue, Fawn, Light Gray, Steel Gray, Sandy, and White.

Even if Flemish Giant rabbits are a fairly new breed, they are now qualified for a rabbit show and it is recognized by the British Rabbit Council (BRC), American Rabbit Breeders Association (ARBA), United States Flemish Giant Rabbit Club as well as international rabbit organizations like the European Confederation of Rabbits, Pigeons and Poultry.

The Flemish Giant rabbit is a very docile, intelligent, friendly creature and a highly trainable breed, this breed also have wide variety of colors and patterns created by breeders and rabbit enthusiasts although only seven are officially recognized. Flemish Giant rabbits are also fond of chewing like any other pets, and they can comprehend certain orders as well. They can even respond to their name which makes them great house pets much like cats and dogs; the only difference is that these rabbits can be high maintenance. They cherish people with whom they form very strong bonds with. They are gentle and understanding and they can are naturally people-oriented.

Proper socialization and training from a young age will help prevent the rabbit from being aggressive to people. Flemish Giants do very well as family pets and they can also be good with children – although may not be recommended for very young children.

The Flemish Giant has a long and powerful body type; they are one of the largest rabbit breed in the world. This breed weighs an average of 14 pounds; the heaviest recorded Flemish Giant reached 21 pounds. They also have bold and bright eyes.

Like any other pets, rabbits also have a great deal of energy and needs daily exercise to work off that energy through the toys that you can provide. It can adapt to almost any kind of environment, they are generally curious yet controllable indoors as long as they get enough mental and physical stimulation during the day and has proper house training as well as litter training.

The average lifespan for the Flemish Giant breed is between 8 and 10 years, longer than the average rabbit breed; the breed is very healthy in general. Like many rabbits, however, the Flemish Giant is prone to health issues such as Calcivirus, Pasteurellosis, Pneumonia, E. Cuniculi, Ringworm, Hepatic and Intestinal Coccidiosis, Abscesses and Urine Burn which will be tackled in the next few chapters later on in this book.

In terms of grooming, the Flemish Giant rabbits have short coats that need to be brushed and groomed at least once a week to keep their coat and skin healthy, a daily brushing may be required for some especially when they are molting.

General Body Types of Rabbits

This section will give you an idea on what kind of body type your Flemish Giant rabbit may have and how you can distinguish it from other kinds of breed. Aside from the ear type, you can also differentiate a rabbit through the type of its fur.

Here are the general body types and shapes of rabbit breeds according to the ARBA:

Full Arch

These rabbits have an arched back that starts at the nape of the neck, arching to the tail.

Semi-Arch (or Mandolin)

Flemish Giant rabbits are classified under this body type; they have an arched back that starts behind the shoulders and arches to the tail. They have a well-defined rise of arch near the shoulders; the highest point of the rise occurs at the top of the hips.

Compact

These rabbits are lighter and shorter in length than meat rabbits, usually kept for show or kept as pets.

Cylindrical

These rabbits have a long, thin, rounded body with small bones and a long, slender head.

Commercial

These are rabbits that are medium in size with bodies about as wide as they are deep.

Types of Rabbit

You can also differentiate a rabbit through their purpose or the reason why they are bred in the first place. It can be shown by the type of their fur or body shape.

Meat Rabbits

These rabbits grow quickly and are usually ready for slaughter by about 8 to 12 weeks of age. Originally, Flemish Giants are bred for its meat.

Fur Rabbits

These rabbits are bred for their soft, thick fur which can be used for coats and trim on clothing. Flemish Giants can also be under this category.

Wool Rabbits

These are rabbits which produce wool in the same way that a sheep produces wool.

Flemish Giant Rabbit Standard Colors

Flemish Giant rabbits come in different colors and patterns. For the most detailed description of these colors and patterns, refer to the breed standards set forth by the ARBA and the BRC.

In this section you will find an overview of the official colors of Flemish Giant rabbits.

- **Black**

  Surface color shall be solid black. The under color shall be slate blue. Eyes should be brown in color.
  Faults: ticking or brownish cast

- **Blue**

  The surface color shall be dark blue. The under color shall be slate blue. Eyes should be blue gray.
  Faults: ticking or brownish cast

- **Fawn**

  The surface color shall be a rich golden straw color. The under color shall blend to a pale cream next to the skin. Belly surface color, undercool and underside of tail shall be light cream to white. Crotch marks are accepted.
  Faults: ticking, excessively wide eye circles, light patches on any part of the body, ear lacing, smut, reddish belly color.

- **Light Gray**

  The surface color shall be a uniform light gray with ticking of black tipped guard hairs. It shall be an agouti coat with distinct bands visible when blowing into the coat. The under color shall be slate blue next to the skin, and there shall be an intermediate band of off white. Belly surface color shall be white with slate blue under color. Crotch marks are accepted. Underside of tail shall be a continuation of belly surface color. Eyes should be brown.

Faults: dark gray belly surface color, sandy or brassiness in surface color.

- **Sandy**

  The surface color shall be a reddish sandy interspersed with contrasting dark ticking. The under color shall show a brassy reddish intermediate color with slate blue under color next to the skin. The ears shall be laced with black. The belly and underside of the tail shall be cream to white except for crotch marks. Eyes should be brown.

  Faults: heavy, dark ticking, smudgy or patchy color, slate blue belly under color is permissible but not desirable.

- **Steel Gray**

  Surface color shall be a black steel gray, with a moderate amount of light gray tipped guard hairs evenly distributed. This color shall be even over the entire body, including head, ears, feet and legs. Under color shall be slate blue, carried down to the skin. Belly surface color shall be white as possible, with slate blue under color. Underside of the tail shall be a continuation of the belly surface color. Crotch marks are accepted. Eyes should be brown.

Faults: Brownish cast, black patches, belly under color similar to balance of body.

- **White**

  Color shall be pure white though out. Eyes should be pink

  Faults: yellow cast; stains

Mane Types of Flemish Giant Rabbits

Now that you understand basic facts about Flemish Giant rabbits, the next you thing need to know is the two types of their manes or the kind of coat they have. In this section you will find a brief overview on how to identify what kind of mane your rabbit has as well as the different colors and patterns of their coats.

Single Mane

Single mane rabbits means that the breed only has one gene that produces the mane or that wooly and thick crimping, that can be found around their ears and chin or in the head, sometimes it can also be seen on the chest and rump area of the rabbit. Flemish Giant rabbits with a mane do not usually hold it for an entire lifetime, for most rabbits their mane usually becomes thin hairs that could disappear or diminishes as they became older.

A purebred double mane rabbit crossbred with another breed can produce a single mane Flemish Giant rabbits or kits. However, some kits are born without a mane gene; it is referred to as "no mane"

Double Mane

If single mane rabbits have one copy of the mane gene, then double mane rabbits obviously have two copies.

The mane thick of wool is usually found around the head and on their flanks which other refer to as a skirt. The double mane rabbit genes are visible when they were born, because you can see a V-form or V-shape area around their flanks or 'skirts.'

If you wanted to have a double maned Flemish Giant rabbit, you should be able to breed a two single maned rabbits or two double maned Flemish Giant rabbits.

History

Flemish Giants are descendants of the extinct European Patagonian and Stone rabbit breed. These rabbits originally came from Flanders Belgium and had been around since the 1860's.

Around the 1890's during the rabbit boom, the breed was imported in United States from Belgium and Great Britain.

In 1893, the first standards of the breed were published in Europe. The Flemish Giant is also an ancestor of many rabbit breeds including the Belgian hare.

In 1910, the Flemish Giant was starting to gain its popularity because it started appearing in rabbit shows and competitions, and in 1915 the National Federation of Flemish Giant Rabbit Breeders (NFFGRB) are founded to promote the breed throughout America and the world.

Around 1924, the American Rabbit Breeders Association (ARBA) was formed and the NFFGRB became a part of it. And in 1929, the ARBA officially recognized the Flemish Giant Rabbits and created breed standards that are eligible for shows.

Today, Flemish Giant rabbits are one of the most popular and admired breeds in United States and Europe. It is continuously gaining popularity among pet owners and rabbit breeders.

Quick Facts

Pedigree: descendants of Patagonian rabbit; large size breed

Group: the British Rabbit Council (BRC), American Rabbit Breeders Association (ARBA), United States Flemish Giant Rabbit Club and the European Confederation of Rabbits, Pigeons and Poultry.

Breed Size: Large and Long

Length: 32 inches (80 cm)

Weight: average of 14 – 20 pounds

Coat Length: short furry coat

Coat Texture: fine, silky, smooth

Color: Black, Blue, Fawn, Light Gray, Steel Gray, Sandy, and White.

Mane: Single or Double

Temperament: docile, gentle, friendly, active

Strangers: may be wary or scared around strangers

Other Rabbits: generally good with other rabbit breeds if properly trained and socialized

Other Pets: friendly with other pets but if not properly introduce may result to potential aggression

Training: intelligent, responsive and very trainable

Exercise Needs: provide toys for mental and physical stimulation

Health Conditions: generally healthy but predisposed to common illnesses such as Urine Burn, Pasteurellosis, Pneumonia, E. Cuniculi, Ringworm, Hepatic and Intestinal Coccidiosis, Abscesses and Calcivirus

Lifespan: average 8 to 10 years

Chapter Two: Flemish Giant Requirements

Are you now thinking of getting a Flemish Giant rabbit? Awesome! After knowing what they are, their behaviors, and how to deal with them, it's time to give you practical tips on what you need to know before buying one.

In this chapter, you will get a whole lot of information on its pros and cons, its average associated costs as well as the licensing you need so that you will be well on your way to becoming a legitimate Flemish Giant rabbit pet owner – should you decide to be one! It's up to you! Read on!

License Requirements

If you are planning to acquire a Flemish Giant rabbit as your pet, there are certain restrictions and regulations that you need to be aware of. Licensing requirements for rabbits varies in different countries, regions, and states.

Here are some things you need to know regarding the acquirement of Flemish Giant rabbits both in United States and in United Kingdom.

United States Licensing for Rabbits

Before you bring home a new pet, it is always a good idea to determine whether there are any laws in your area which require you to register or license your pet. In many cases, a license or permit is only required for exotic or endangered animals – Flemish Giant rabbits do not qualify. There are, however, some local regulations which may require you to license your rabbit. For example, the state of Minnesota requires rabbit owners to license their pets at $15 a year – the cost may be higher if the rabbit is not spayed or neutered.

If you plan to breed and sell rabbits, you may be subject to an entirely different set of regulations. According to the Animal and Plant Health Inspection Service (APHIS) Animal Welfare Act, your business must be licensed unless you are only selling rabbits for meat or fiber. If you sell rabbits as pets, you do not need a license if your annual sales are under $500. As always, however, it is a good idea to research the regulations in your area before you do anything – it is better to be safe than sorry.

United Kingdom Licensing for Rabbits

Licensing regulations in the U.K. are always a bit different from the United States. For example, rabbit owners are not required to obtain a license or permit for their rabbits. If you plan to import a rabbit from outside the U.K. or export one outside the country, however, you will need to obtain an animal movement license (AML). This rule is in place because rabies has been eradicated from the U.K. and unregulated imports and exports of live animals could re-introduce the disease.

How Many Flemish Giant Rabbits Should You Keep?

For the most part, rabbits are naturally very social creatures so they enjoy being kept with other rabbits. It is not necessarily a requirement that you keep two of the same kind of rabbit either – as long as they are similar in size and their cage provides ample space for both, you can keep different breeds of Flemish Giant rabbits together. The best way to ensure harmony among your rabbits is to raise them together from a young age – ideally younger than 12 weeks.

Ideally one or two Flemish Giant rabbits are fine; just make sure that before you get another one, you can provide for the needs of both rabbits.

If you keep more than two rabbits together, make sure there is no more than one male for every two females. The best combination is an altered male and female pair or a pair of brothers or sisters.

Do Flemish Giant Rabbits Get Along with Other Pets?

They may or may not get along that's for sure; there are many factors to consider like their individual temperament. Their tempers vary from one rabbit to another – some rabbits might be very docile and unflappable while others may be a little more nervous and high-strung. You also have to consider the temperament of your dog or cat. Some pets have a very low prey drive so you don't really have to worry about them chasing your rabbit around. Other breeds, however, particularly terriers and other hunting breeds, have a very high prey drive and if your rabbit has a high flight response, it could lead to a dangerous chase.

When it comes to Flemish Giant rabbits getting along with cats, the response is also highly varied. Younger Flemish Giant rabbits may look more like prey to a cat than an adult or full grown rabbit. If your rabbit is larger than your cat, it probably won't be a problem but you still need to be careful. The best thing to do is to introduce your pets to each other while they are still young so they grow up together. Even then, you should still supervise their interactions to be safe.

Ease and Cost of Care

Owning a Flemish Giant rabbit doesn't come cheap! The fact is that, these rabbits require maintenance which means that you have to provide supplies and be able to cover the expenses in order to maintain a healthy lifestyle and environment for your pet.

These things will definitely add up to your daily budget, and the cost will vary depending on where you buy it; the brand of the accessories, the nutrients included in its food and the time being. If you want to seriously own a Flemish Giant rabbit as a pet you should be able to cover the necessary costs it entails.

In this section you will receive an overview of the expenses associated with purchasing and keeping a Flemish Giant rabbit such as food and treats, grooming and cleaning supplies, toys, and regular veterinary care. You will receive an overview of these costs as well as an estimate for each in the following pages of this section.

Initial Costs

The initial costs for keeping a Flemish Giant rabbit include those costs that you must cover before you can bring your rabbit home. Some of the initial costs you will need to cover include your rabbit's cage, food and water equipment, toys and accessories, initial vaccinations, spay/neuter surgery and supplies for grooming, bathing and nail clipping not to mention the cost of the rabbit itself. You will find an overview of each of these costs as well as an estimate for each below:

Purchase Price: $50 - $150

The cost to purchase a Flemish Giant rabbit can vary greatly depending on the breed, where you buy him and whether it was pedigreed or not. You can probably find a backyard breeder offering $50 or below, but you cannot be sure of the breeding quality for these rabbits. Generally speaking, pet-quality Flemish Giant rabbits sell for $50 to $150, maybe even more. If you want to invest in a show-quality rabbit, you may have to pay a much higher price – usually as much as $200 depending on the breeder.

Cage or Hutch: $35 - $120

When it comes to rabbit cages or pets in general, bigger is better! Rabbits are fairly active animals so they need a cage or hutch large enough that they have space to move around. It is also a good idea to let your rabbit out of the cage on a daily basis, but the cage still needs to be fairly large. The cost of the cage highly depends on its size, and the materials from which it is made.

Food and Water Bowls: average of $20

In addition to providing your Flemish Giant rabbit with a cage or hutch, you should also make sure he has a set of high-quality food bowls and a water bottle. The best materials food bowls is stainless steel because it is easy to clean and doesn't harbor bacteria – ceramic is another good option. The average cost for a quality stainless steel bowl and a rabbit water bottle is about $20. Depending on the brand, some equipment could cost more than the average.

Toys: $50 and up

You need to buy quality toys for your rabbit because these toys help to provide your pet with mental and physical stimulation to prevent boredom. Many toys can also be used as chew toys to help wear down your rabbit's teeth. You might want to start off with an assortment of different toys to see which kind your rabbit likes. Plan to budget a cost of around $50 for toys just to be sure you have enough.

Initial Vaccinations: $20 and up

Rabbits don't need as many vaccinations as cats and dogs, but they should be vaccinated for calcivirus around 12 weeks of age. Your veterinarian can tell you if your rabbit needs any other vaccinations. To cover the cost of these vaccinations you should budget about $20 or more just to be prepared.

Spay/Neuter Surgery: $50 - $150

If you don't plan to breed your Flemish Giant rabbit you should seriously consider having him or her neutered or spayed. Unfortunately, the cost to spay or neuter a large breed is fairly high – around $50 to $150. However, if you keep two rabbits of the same sex together, it may not be necessary.

Supplies/Accessories: $50

In addition to purchasing your rabbit's cage and other accessories, you should also purchase some basic grooming supplies like nail clippers, a brush, and mild antiseptic ear-cleaning solution. You should also purchase a litter box if you want to litter train your rabbit. The cost for these items will vary depending on the quality and also quantity, so you should budget about $50 or more for these extra costs.

Needs	Costs
Purchase Price	$50 - $150 (£39.78 - £119.34)
Cage or Hutch	$35 to $120 (£28.04 to £96.13)
Food/Water Equipment	$20 (£16.02)
Toys	$50 (£40.06)
Vaccinations	$20 (£16.02)
Spay/Neuter	$50 to $150 (£40.06 to £120.17)
Accessories	$50 (£40.06)
Total	$275 to $375 (£218.78 – £298.34)

*Costs may vary depending on location
**Costs may change based on the currency exchange

Monthly Costs

The monthly costs for keeping a Flemish Giant rabbit as a pet include those costs which recur on a monthly basis. The most important monthly cost for keeping a rabbit is, of course, food. In addition to food, however, you'll also need to think about things like your bedding, litter, toy replacements, and veterinary exams. Here is the overview of each of these costs as well as an estimate for each need.

Food and Treats: $25 - $30

Feeding your Flemish Giant rabbit a healthy diet is very important for his health and wellness. Rabbits usually eat about 1 ounce of food per pound of bodyweight, so you can expect a 5-pound rabbit to eat about 9 pounds of food per month. Rabbit pellets usually cost about $8 or so for 5 pounds of food.

For a Flemish Giant rabbit, you should budget about $25 per month for food; usually a full grown Flemish Giant will eat about 2 cups of pellets a day on average depending on the rabbit's appetite and size. You should also provide your rabbit with fresh hay and vegetables which can cost an extra $10 a month or so.

Bedding and Litter: around $20

Whether or not you need bedding for your rabbit cage will depend on the type of cage you use. Even if you don't use bedding in the whole cage, you should still provide some kind of hideaway lined with comfy bedding for your Flemish Giant rabbit to sleep in.

It is also recommended that you replace your rabbit's litter once in a while. You should plan to spend about $20 a month on bedding and litter for your rabbit cage.

Veterinary Exams: average of $7

In order to keep your rabbit healthy you should take him to the veterinarian about every six months or so. The average cost for a vet visit for a rabbit is about $40 or more, if you have two visits per year, it averages to about $7 per month.

Other Costs: around $15

In addition to the monthly costs for your rabbit's food, bedding, litter, and vet visits there are also some other cost you might have to pay occasionally. These costs might include things like replacements for worn-out toys as well as cleaning products. You should budget about $15 per month for extra costs.

Needs	Costs
Food and Treats	$25 to $30 (£16.02 to £24.03)
Bedding/Litter	$20 (£16.02)
Veterinary Exams	$7 (£5.61)
Other Costs	$15 (£12.02)
Total	$67 to $72 (£53.30 to £57.28)

*Costs may vary depending on location
**Costs may change based on the currency exchange

Pros and Cons of Flemish Giant Rabbits

Before you bring a Flemish Giant rabbit home you should take the time to learn the pros and cons of the breed. Every rabbit breed is different so you need to think about the details to determine whether the Flemish Giant rabbit is actually the right pet for you.

In this section you will find a list of pros and cons for the Flemish Giant rabbit breed:

Pros for Flemish Giant Rabbits

- Flemish Giant rabbits come in a variety of colors depending on the breed which allows you to choose the best option.
- They are active but can be controlled indoors
- Flemish Giant rabbits are easily trained to use a litter box - makes it easy to clean up after them.
- Generally a friendly, docile pet as long as there is proper introduction or socialization at a young age.
- Flemish Giant rabbits are easy to care for in terms of their diet – they eat mainly pellets, hay, and fresh veggies.
- Flemish Giant rabbits do not require regular grooming because of their short coat

Cons for Flemish Giant Rabbits

- Flemish Giants are cute but it can be a high maintenance pet since it is a large breed
- Generally a good pet but may not be advisable for small living spaces such as condos and apartments.
- Rabbits cannot be kept in their cages 24/7 – they need space and time to explore.
- May not be a good choice for a household that already has cats and/or rabbits.

- Generally not recommended for very young children who don't know how to handle a rabbit.
- Can be a long-term commitment – most rabbits live anywhere from 8 to 12 years.
- Cost for maintenance will definitely be additional expense.

Chapter Three: Purchasing Your Flemish Giant Rabbit

Now that you are already aware and have prior knowledge about the legal aspects of owning and maintaining a Flemish Giant rabbit as well as its pros and cons, the next step is purchasing one through a local pet store or a legitimate breeder. In this chapter you will find valuable information about where to find a Flemish Giant rabbit breeder, how to select a reputable breeder, and how to choose a healthy buck or doe (baby rabbit) from a litter. You will also receive tips for your home and for introducing your new Flemish Giant rabbit to your family.

Choosing a Reputable Flemish Giant Rabbit Breeder

To make sure that you get a well-bred, healthy Flemish Giant rabbit of your chosen breed, your best bet is to look around for a local breeder. You can feel free to ask around at your local pet store and you may also be able to get a personal recommendation from friends or your local veterinarian. Once you have your list of breeders on hand you can go through them one-by-one to narrow down your options.

Here are the following guidelines for you to be able to choose a reputable rabbit breeder:

Do a Background Check

Visit the website for each breeder on your list (if they have one) and look for key information about the breeder's history and experience.

- Check for ARBA or BRC registrations and a license, if applicable.
- If the website doesn't provide any information about the facilities or the breeder you are best just moving on.

Interview the Breeders

Now that you have narrowed down some breeders, contact the remaining breeders on your list by phone

- Ask the breeder questions about his experience with breeding rabbits in general and about the specific Flemish Giant rabbit breed you are looking for.
- Ask for information about the breeding stock including registration numbers and health information.
- Expect a reputable breeder to ask you questions about yourself as well – a responsible breeder wants to make sure that his rabbits go to good homes.

Do an Onsite Inspection

Schedule an appointment to visit the facilities for the remaining breeders on your list after you've weeded a few more of them out.

- Ask for a tour of the facilities, including the place where the breeding stock is kept as well as the facilities housing the baby rabbits.

- If things look unorganized or unclean, do not purchase from the breeder.

- Make sure the breeding stock is in good condition and that the baby rabbits are all healthy-looking and active.

Select Your Breeder

By this time you should have narrowed down the best of the best breeders on your list, before making a decision consider every factor to make the most out of it. Make sure the breeder provides some kind of health guarantee and ask about any vaccinations the rabbits may already have. Put down a deposit, if needed, to reserve a rabbit if they aren't ready to come home yet.

List of Breeders and Rescue Websites

There are so many Flemish Giant rabbit breeds to choose from, that's why you need to do some research and decide which breed you want before you start shopping around. When you are ready to buy a Flemish Giant rabbit, you then need to start thinking about where you are going to get it. You may be able to find a Flemish Giant rabbit at your local pet store, but think carefully before you buy whether that is really the best option. When you buy a rabbit from a pet store you have no way of knowing where the rabbit came from – you also don't know anything about the quality of its breeding.

If you want a baby rabbit, your best chance is to find a local Flemish Giant rabbit breeder. Before you go down that road, however, consider whether adopting an adult rabbit might be the better option for you. There are plenty of adult rabbits out there who have been abandoned by their previous owners and they are looking for a new forever home. When you adopt a rabbit you are actually saving a life and there are some benefits for you as well!

Adopting a rabbit can sometimes be cheaper than buying from a breeder and, in many cases you get a cage and accessories with the adoption. Many adult rabbits ready for adoption have also already been spayed or neutered, litter trained, and they will be caught up on vaccinations.

Here is the list of breeders and adoption rescue websites around United States and United Kingdom:

United States Breeders and Rescue Websites

Rabbit Breeders
<http://rabbitbreeders.us/flemish-giant-rabbit-breeders>

Double L Rabbit Ranch

<http://www.llrabbitranch.com/sale>

Sugar Rays Rabbits

<http://sugarraysrabbits.tripod.com/index.html>

Flemish Giant Rabbit Breeders List

<http://www.crystalcreekrabbits.com/>

Tiffany's Rabbitry

<http://www.flemishgiant.net/rabbit-home-page/>

Crystal Creek Rabbits

<http://www.crystalcreekrabbits.com/>

A & K Ranch Beefalo

<http://www.splitlimbranch.com/flemishgiantrabbits.htm>

Overstock Adoption

<https://pets.overstock.com/pets/Other,Flemish-Giant,/species,breed,/?distance=25>

BunSpace Rabbit Rescue

<http://www.bunspace.com/>

Erie Area Rabbit Society and Rescue

<http://www.eriearearabbitsociety.org/>

Long Island Rabbit Rescue Group.

<http://www.longislandrabbitrescue.org/happy_tails.htm>

Magic Happens Rabbit Rescue

<http://www.magichappensrescue.com/>

The Bunny Bunch Rescue

<http://www.bunnybunch.org/pages/>

Disabled Rabbits Rescue

<http://www.disabledrabbits.com/adopt.html>

United Kingdom Breeders and Rescue Websites

Rabbit Rehome Adoption

<http://www.rabbitrehome.org.uk/search/breed/giant>

Southampton Rabbit Rescue

<http://www.southamptonrabbitrescue.org.uk/>

Cotton Tails Rescue

<http://www.cottontails-rescue.org.uk/>

The Cat & Rabbit Rescue Centre

<http://www.crrc.co.uk/>

Fairly Beloved Rabbit Care

<http://www.fbrc.org.uk/>

Acomb Rabbit Rescue

<http://www.acombrabbitrescue.org.uk/>

British Giant Rabbits

<http://www.british-giantrabbits.co.uk/>

Pets 4 Homes UK

<http://www.pets4homes.co.uk/pets4homes/home.nsf/rabbit
ssale!openform&Breed=Flemish>

FreeAds UK

<http://www.freeads.co.uk/uk/buy-sell/pets/rabbits/Flemish
Giant/#.WDzm9NJ97Dc>

Selecting a Healthy Flemish Giant Rabbit

After you have narrowed down your list of options to just two or three Flemish Giant rabbit breeders, your next step is to actually pick out the baby rabbit you want. You have already determined that the remaining breeders on your list are responsible, but now you need to make sure that the baby rabbits they have available are healthy and ready to go home with their new owners.

Here are some few guidelines to keep in mind when selecting a healthy rabbit:

- **Check the Environment of the Rabbits**

 Ask the breeder to give you a tour of the facilities. Make sure the facilities where the rabbits are housed is clean and sanitary – if there is evidence of diarrhea, do not purchase one of the rabbits because they may already be sick.

- **Observe the Rabbits' Behaviors**

 Take a few minutes to observe the litter as a whole, watching how the rabbits interact with each other. The baby rabbits should be active and playful, interacting with each other in a healthy way. Avoid any rabbits that appear to be lethargic and those that have difficulty moving – they could be sick.

- **Interact with the Rabbits**

Put your hand into the cage or nesting box and give the baby rabbits time to sniff and explore you before you interact with them. Pet the baby rabbits and encourage them to play with a toy, taking the opportunity to observe their personalities. Then you can single out any of the rabbits that you think might be a good fit and spend a little more time with them.

You can also pick up the baby rabbit and hold him to see how he responds to human contact. The baby rabbit might squirm a little but it shouldn't be frightened of you and it should enjoy being pet.

- **Examine the Rabbits Body**

Examine the rabbit's body for signs of any illness and potential injury.

Eyes: The baby rabbit should have clear, bright eyes with no discharge.

Ears: Their ears should be clean and clear with no discharge or inflammation.

Body: The baby rabbit stomach may be round but it shouldn't be distended or swollen.

Mobility: The baby rabbit should be able to walk and run normally without any mobility problems.

Chapter Four: Caring for Your Flemish Giant Rabbit

The Flemish Giant rabbit makes a wonderful pet largely because of his energetic yet docile personality, but these rabbits are also very adaptable to different types of living situations. In this chapter you will learn the basics about your rabbit's habitat requirements including the recommended cage type, useful accessories, and exercise requirements. You will also receive tips for litter training and for taming and handling your Flemish Giant rabbit.

Habitat Requirements for Flemish Giant Rabbits

Unlike other rabbits the Flemish Giant definitely needs a cage to run around freely. They are quite high maintenance because of their size especially when they became adults. But aside from space, the main thing your rabbit needs in terms of its habitat is lots of love and affection from his human companions and adequate exercise. Rabbits are a cuddly and loving breed that bonds closely with family, so you should make an effort to spend some quality time with your Flemish Giant each and every day. If your pet doesn't get enough attention he may be more likely to develop problem behaviors like chewing house furniture and potential aggression as well as separation anxiety.

In addition to playing with your rabbit and spending time with him every day, you also need to make sure that his needs for exercise are met. Rabbits are a very active creature that's why it's important for you to also make sure your pet gets plenty of mental stimulation from interactive toys and games.

Keep reading to learn the basics about your rabbit's habitat requirements. You will also learn about recommended cage accessories and receive tips for choosing the right bedding for your rabbit as well as some guidelines on how to handle and tame your pet.

Ideal Rabbit Cage

When it comes to choosing a cage for your rabbit there are several things to consider. Here are the following things you should keep in mind:

- **Cage Size**

First thing you need to prioritize is the size of the cage. Rabbits are active animals so even if you let your rabbit out of the cage sometimes his cage should still be large enough so that he can move around with ease. At the least, your rabbit cage should be 4 to 6 times the length of your rabbit when he is fully stretched out. Take the time to at least have an estimate measurement of your rabbit's body because its size may also depend on their age or breed. Flemish Giants are quite larger than normal rabbits so you might want to buy something bigger so that it can fit even if he becomes a full adult. Ideally the recommended cage requirement is 24 x 36 x48 or an XL size similar to a dog crate with litter pan and bed.

- **Cage Materials**

Another factor you need to consider with your rabbit's cage is the materials from which it is made. You want to choose a cage that is easy to clean and can be durable. Wooden cages are not advisable because it absorbs moisture and harbor bacteria. Generally speaking, plastic cages and metal cages are usually the best choice. Avoid cages with wire flooring, however, because these can irritate your rabbit's feet. If you have to choose a cage with a wire floor, cover a portion of it with a square of carpet or a mat – otherwise your rabbit will probably just hang out in his litter box.

- **'Play Space' or Pen Space**

If you don't want to let your rabbit run loose in the house, you should provide an exercise pen in addition to a large cage. The cage itself should provide at least 8 square feet of space for 1 to 2 rabbits and the exercise space should provide at least 24 square feet of space. Bigger is better especially for the Flemish Giant breed. Your rabbit should get at least 5 hours a day in the exercise pen or, if you are handy, you can connect the pen to his cage so he can come and go as he pleases.

Indoor Cages vs. Outdoor Hutches

It is not wise if you keep you rabbits outdoors, although many rabbit owners think that rabbits are best kept in outdoor hutches, but this may not necessarily be the case. There are, however, some important pros and cons to consider for outdoor rabbits. For example, it is easier to find space for a very large cage to house multiple rabbits outdoors – you also don't have to worry about noise or odors if you keep your rabbits outdoors. If you provide your rabbits with an outdoor run, they will be able to eat grass and other plants to supplement their diet without costing you any extra money. Plus, clean-up is easier for outdoor cages than for indoor cages.

On the other side of the issue, keeping rabbits outdoors may expose them to parasites and other dangerous diseases – especially if they come into contact with wild rabbits. If your rabbits are kept outdoors, they may not receive as much attention and human interaction as they might if they were kept inside. Keeping your rabbits outdoors puts them at risk for predation and they could also be exposed to extreme temperatures and inclement weather which could make them sick.

Recommended Cage Accessories

In addition to providing your rabbit with a cage, you also need to stock it with certain accessories. Here are a few things your rabbit needs for its cage:

- **Water bottle**

When it comes to your rabbit's water bottle, it is worth it to spend a few extra dollars for a non-drip model – this will keep you from having to change your bedding as frequently.

- **Food Bowl**

Food and water dishes for rabbits come in all shapes and sizes but you should choose a set that suits your pet's needs. Flemish Giant rabbits are relatively large breeds, so don't choose anything too small. As mentioned in the previous chapters, stainless steel and ceramic bowls do not harbor bacteria like plastic can and they are easy to clean.

- **Hay Rack**

It is recommended that you buy a hay rack to keep your rabbit's hay fresh by raising it up off the floor of the cage where it could be soiled.

- **Litter Pan**

Your rabbit's litter pan does not need to be anything fancy – it just needs to be large enough for your rabbit to turn around in and deep enough to contain the litter without making it hard for your rabbit to get into the pan.

- **Toys**

As mentioned earlier your rabbit also needs toys to prevent it from getting bored plus it also a form of exercise. You may want to buy chew toys and other types to provide mental and physical stimulation. It is ideal that you buy an assortment of toys at first and give your rabbit time to play with them so you can learn which type of toys he prefers.

- **Bedding**

Your rabbit also needs a hiding place or shelter and of course a bedding. You may need to consider the type of litter you want to use for your rabbit's bedding – if you choose to use any at all. The best litter to use in a rabbit cage is fresh hay – ideally edible hay like meadow hay or timothy hay. You can also use a blanket made from some kind of natural fiber.

Straw bedding and shredded newspaper or cardboard is not recommended for rabbit cages because it absorbs moisture which can lead to urine burn and it can also harbor bacteria. The worst bedding for rabbits is wood shavings, sawdust, cat litter, or any kind of cedar or pine product.

Litter Training Your Rabbit

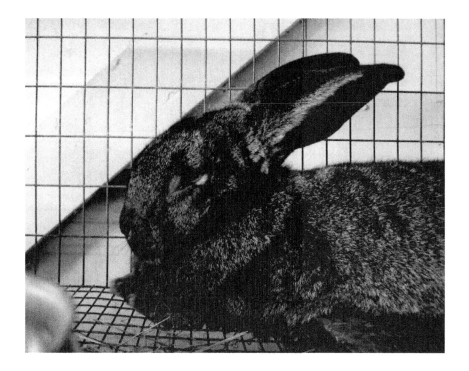

Once you have set up your rabbit's cage, your next step is to litter train your rabbit. Rabbits are naturally fairly clean animals and they tend to choose one or two places in their cage to urinate and defecate. This makes your job very easy. All you have to do is watch your rabbit for a few days to determine where he tends to relieve himself and then simply place a litter pan in that area. Some rabbits choose a single location and others choose two or more – they are usually located in the corners of cage.

After discovering where your rabbit likes to relieve himself, you need to determine which type of litter you want to use. Avoid cat litters because they are often dusty or scented – you also don't want anything that clumps. The best litter to use is something organic made from alfalfa or oat hay, even paper. You can also simply use fresh hay as your litter! You want to avoid wood shavings, sawdust, and shredded newspaper or cardboard because they can absorb moisture. You also want to avoid anything made with cedar or pine because the natural oils can irritate your rabbit.

Handling and Taming Your Rabbit

At some point in time, you and your pet will already get along and are comfortable in each other, strengthen your relationship by taming them through training. Training a rabbit is not that hard to do, in fact it can be a fun and rewarding bonding experience for both of you.

There are lots of pet owners out there who have properly trained and raised a well-behaved Flemish Giant rabbit. They are easy to tame, that is why they can absorb information very quickly and easily as long as you do it right. Trust is the most important key in taming your rabbits. The first thing you need to do is to be able to establish a solid connection and rapport between you and your pet.

This section will provide some guidelines you can do

to get your rabbit well-behaved and disciplined. Are you ready? Read on!

Rabbits make wonderful pets for a number of reasons but one of those reasons is that they are easy to tame. The more time you spend with your rabbit, the more quickly he will get used to you and he will come to enjoy interacting with you. It is important to remember, however, that rabbits are fragile animals so you want to be careful about how you handle them. You must also remember that rabbits are prey animals so they dislike being picked up – if you do pick your rabbit up, hold him securely against your chest until you can sit down then place him on your lap.

If you are a new rabbit owner, it may take some practice to learn how to safely pick your rabbit up out of his cage. One thing you can do is use small treats to entice your rabbit to come to you. When he does, start gently petting him along the back until he seems calm enough for you to pick him up. When you do, make sure to support his body from underneath and then hold him securely against your chest to make sure he doesn't fall.

Chapter Five: Meeting Your Rabbit's Nutritional Needs

Feeding your Flemish Giant rabbit is not that complicated. However, its level of activity should be taken into consideration to meet its nutritional diet. Rabbits, like many other pets, should be given the right amount of recommended food for a balanced nutrition because proper diet can lengthen the life expectancy of your rabbit.

In this section, you'll learn the majority of your pet's nutritional needs as well as feeding tips and foods that are good and harmful.

The Nutritional Needs of Rabbits

Rabbits are herbivores which mean that the entirety of their diet should be made up of plant products. It is also important to realize that rabbits have very high needs for fiber in their diet. Making sure that your rabbit's nutritional needs are met is actually quite simple – a balanced diet for rabbits should be made up of high-quality commercial pellets, fresh timothy hay, oat hay, and fresh vegetables. Your rabbit also needs constant access to fresh water because this too plays a role in your rabbit's digestion. Here are the food you should feed your

- **Commercial Pellets**

When choosing a high-quality commercial pellet to use as your rabbit's staple diet, there are a few things you should look for. First of all, the pellets should contain at least 18% fiber – the more the better. And make sure that the pellets you are buying are fresh. Do not purchase more than your rabbit can eat in 6 weeks' time because that is about as long as the pellets will remain fresh. After that point, they will lose some of their nutritional value and they won't provide your rabbit with the nutrients he needs.

- **Grass Hays**

Aside from choosing a quality pellet for your rabbit you should also stock up on fresh grass hay. Grass hay is loaded with calcium, vitamin A, vitamin D and other nutrients plus, the process of eating hay helps to keep your rabbit's digestive tract healthy and also helps to wear down his teeth. Your rabbit needs at least one type of grass hay – timothy hay is generally the easiest and most cost-effective option to find. He also needs some oat hay. Alfalfa hay is okay for young rabbits because it contains more protein than other hays but it should only be offered occasionally for adult rabbits because fiber is more important for them than protein. Like the pellets, you want to make sure that your hay stays fresh.

- **Fresh Vegetables**

Last but definitely not the least is fresh vegetables. You should aim to feed your rabbit about 1 cup of leafy greens per 2 pounds of bodyweight per day with a fair amount of other vegetables – leafy greens are nutrient-dense and should comprise about 75% of your rabbit's fresh vegetable intake. Leafy greens include things like spinach, parsley, mustard greens, swiss chard, arugula, lettuce, dandelion greens, cilantro, and more.

Here is a list of non-leafy green vegetables that are also safe for rabbits:

- Carrots
- Broccoli
- Edible flowers
- Celery
- Bell peppers
- Snow peas

- Brussel sprouts
- Cabbage (any type)
- Broccolini
- Summer squash
- Zucchini
- Wheat grass

- **Fresh Fruits**

In addition to fresh vegetables, you can also feed your rabbit small amounts of fresh fruit – these should comprise no more than 10% of your rabbit's fresh diet. Feed your rabbit no more than 1 teaspoon per 2 pounds of bodyweight on a daily basis. Below are the list of fruits that are safe for Flemish Giant rabbits:

- Banana
- Melons
- Star Fruit
- Apricot
- Currants
- Nectarines
- Apple
- Cherries

- Pear
- Peach
- Plum
- Kiwi
- Papaya
- Mango
- Berries
- Pineapple

Important Reminder

When feeding your Flemish Giant rabbit fresh fruits and vegetables, make sure you don't go overboard with the portions and make sure to introduce new foods slowly. Always keep an eye on your rabbit's digestion to make sure he tolerates the new foods well. Consult your veterinarian if he your pet develops any kind of digestive problems after feeding him a new food.

Toxic Foods to Avoid

It might be tempting to give in to your rabbit when he is at the table, but certain "people foods" can actually be toxic for your pet. As a general rule, you should never feed your rabbit anything unless you are 100% sure that it is safe.

In this section you will find a list of foods that can be toxic to rabbits and should therefore be avoided.

- Avocado
- Beets
- Bread
- Chocolate
- Coffee
- Citrus peels
- Corn
- Fresh peas
- Grains
- Green beans
- Legumes
- Nuts
- Onions
- Potatoes

- Rice
- Rhubarb leaves
- Seeds
- Sugar

If your rabbit eats any of these foods, contact the Pet Poison Control hotline right away at (888) 426 – 4435.

Tips for Feeding Flemish Giant Rabbits

Now that you know what to feed your Flemish Giant rabbit you may be wondering when and how much to feed him. To make sure that your rabbit gets the nutrients he needs, you need to adjust his diet based on his age. For example, baby rabbits that have just been weaned can benefit from higher protein content in their diet while adult rabbits need more fiber than protein.

Here's an overview of the ideal composition of a Flemish Giant rabbit's diet as determined by his or her age:

Baby Rabbits (Birth to 7 months)

- **From birth to 3 weeks** – mother's milk only
- **From 3 to 4 weeks** – mother's milk, small portions of pellets and alfalfa hay

- **From 4 to 7 weeks** – mother's milk, free access to pellets and alfalfa hay
- **From 7 weeks to 12 weeks** - unlimited access to pellets and alfalfa hay
- **From 12 weeks to 7 months** – introduce veggies one at a time, unlimited access to pellets and alfalfa hay

Young Adult Rabbits (7 months to 12 months)

- Introduce timothy hay, grass hay, oat hay, and other hays while decreasing alfalfa hay
- Decrease pellet consumption to ½ cup per 6 pounds of bodyweight
- Increase daily consumption of vegetables to 1 cup per 6 pounds of bodyweight
- Introduce fruit in small quantities – no more than 1 to 2 ounces per 6 pounds bodyweight

Mature Adult Rabbits (1 year to 5 years)

- Unlimited daily access to timothy hay, oat hay, and other grass hays
- Decrease to ¼ to ½ cup pellets per 6 pounds bodyweight
- At least 2 cups fresh veggies per 6 pounds bodyweight daily
- Fruit ration no more than 2 ounces (about 2 tbsp.) per 6 pounds bodyweight daily
-

Senior Rabbits (6 years and older)

- Continue adult diet as long as healthy weight is maintained
- Offer unlimited access to pellets if needed to keep weight up
- Offer alfalfa hay to underweight rabbits as long as calcium levels are within the normal range

Chapter Six: Breeding Your Flemish Giant Rabbit

Nothing is more adorable than a little baby Flemish Giant rabbit – except for maybe a whole litter of them! If you decided to buy two rabbits, for instance a male and female and keep them together, you should definitely prepare for the possibility of breeding, unless it's the same gender, otherwise you're going to be caught off guard! If you are interested in breeding your Flemish Giant rabbit, this chapter will give you a wealth of information about the processes and phases of its breeding and you will also learn how to properly raise bunnies on your own.

This not for everyone but if you want to have better understanding about how to raise these rabbits, then you should definitely not miss this part! On the contrary if you are interested in becoming a reputable breeder, then this is a must read chapter for you.

Basic Rabbit Breeding Information

Before you can breed your Flemish Giant rabbit, you need to understand the basics of rabbit breeding. Most rabbits are mature enough to be mated by the time they reach 4 to 4 ½ months old. Keep in mind large breeds like the Flemish Giant becomes sexually mature at around 6 – 7

months old especially the bucks (male rabbits). However, for the health and safety of your doe (female rabbit), it is recommended that you wait until female Flemish Giant rabbits of are about 9 months to 1 year old before you start breeding them. You can always ask your veterinarian if you aren't sure about your specific Flemish Giant rabbit.

Mating Behavior of Rabbits

When your Flemish Giant rabbits are old enough for breeding, you can introduce the male and female to encourage mating.

The best practice is to take the doe (the female) to the male's cage. If you do it the other way around the buck will probably waste time marking his territory in the new cage and the doe may even become aggressive and territorial toward him. Once you introduce the female to the male's cage, it shouldn't be long before he makes a brief display of courtship behavior and then mounts the female. When the male grunts and falls backward or to the side, you know that the mating has been completed successfully.

To increase the chances of pregnancy, many Flemish Giant rabbit breeders choose to mate their rabbits a second time after one hour. Other breeders prefer to breed the same pair about 24 hours later. It is up to you what kind of schedule you want to follow, but your chances of success will be higher if you allow the pair to mate more than once. If you have multiple female rabbits you want to breed, you may really only need one buck, though it couldn't hurt to have a backup. Just be careful about choosing your pairings because you don't want to engage in any inbreeding.

How to Know if Your Rabbit is Pregnant:

You won't be able to tell immediately whether your Flemish Giant rabbit doe is pregnant. You should be able to palpate her abdomen and feel the kits by about 14 days after mating. However, you can determine if she is, by doing the following steps, as a caution, be very careful as you do this to avoid harming the kits:

- Hold the doe down gently with one hand and use the other to feel the belly just in front of the pelvis area.
- If the doe is pregnant you should be able to feel several marble-sized embryos.
- If the doe is not pregnant you can rebreed her and check again after 2 weeks.
- If the doe is pregnant, wait about two weeks before adding a nesting box to the cage.

Nesting Requirements

After mating, the nesting box should be provided for your doe Flemish Giant rabbit at about day 28, about 3 days before you can expect her to give birth. There is no reason to place the nesting box any earlier because the rabbit will either use it as a litter box or mess around with it so much that you need to replace the bedding. The nesting box minimum requirement is about 24 x 30 x36. Cut the front with a V-shape or taper it down to about 6 inches so the do can easily climb in and out.

To prevent moisture buildup in the nesting box, keep the top open and line the bottom with ¼-inch mesh. Fill the nesting ox with soft straw, pine shavings, or hay. As long as you add the nesting box about 3 days before delivery, the doe will pull out her own hair and add it to the bedding to make a soft nest for her young.

Labor Process of Flemish Giant Rabbits

The doe should give birth somewhere between 28 and 31 days after mating. Flemish Giant rabbits usually have 5 to 12 kits, although litters can either produce small or large litters.

As soon as the kits are all born you need to check the litter and make sure to remove any that are still-born. Flemish Giant rabbits are quite small when they are born and because they have no hair and closed eyes, they are completely dependent on their mother. Their fur will start to grow in after 5 or 6 days and they will open their eyes after about 10 to 12 days. Sometimes the kits will have crust over their eyes that prevent them from opening – just wipe them carefully with a damp cloth.

Raising Baby Rabbits

Unfortunately, the mortality rate for baby rabbits is fairly high – around 40%. To help reduce this number you should keep the nest box clean and dry. There is no need to clean the box after the first week, but do keep an eye out to make sure it doesn't get too damp or dirty. You should also be mindful about feeding your doe a healthy diet so the nutrients are passed on to her kits. Do not be surprised if the doe spends most of her time out of the nesting box – she will generally only return to feed the kits two or three times a day. After 3 weeks of this, the kits will start to leave the nesting box on their own.

Once your litter of kits has started to leave the nest box, you can think about rebreeding your doe. Does typically reduce their milk production at the 3-week mark but if you breed the doe again about 2 to 3 weeks after kindling you can extend milk production and start weaning the kits at about 4 weeks old. Just keep a close eye on the health and wellness of your doe and your kits to determine the best course of action.

Chapter Seven: Grooming Your Flemish Giant Rabbit

Different Flemish Giant rabbit breeds have different coat lengths and textures so take the time to explore your rabbit's coat in order to determine what his grooming needs might be. Grooming your rabbit helps to distribute its natural body oils to keep his skin healthy, shiny, and soft. No matter what kind of coat your Flemish Giant rabbit has, it is your job to groom it properly so it remains in good health. In this chapter you will learn the basics about grooming your Flemish Giant rabbit – this includes brushing and bathing your rabbit as well as trimming his nails, cleaning his ears, and brushing his teeth.

Recommended Tools to Have on Hand

In order to keep your rabbit's coat clean and in good condition you will need to have a few grooming tools on hand. The most important thing you are going to need is a good brush. The type of brush you need will depend on which kind of Flemish Giant rabbit you have and which type of coat he has either single mane or double mane.

Here are some of the grooming tools that may come in handy when it comes to grooming your Flemish Giant rabbit:

- Slicker brush (no metal teeth)
- Wire-pin brush
- Wide-toothed comb
- Small, sharp scissors
- Nail clippers
- Flea comb
- Styptic powder
- Cotton balls
- Mild antiseptic solution

Learning how to groom your rabbit effectively is a task that takes time to learn. If you have no idea where to start, it wouldn't be a bad idea to talk to a fellow rabbit owner or take your rabbit to a professional groomer so they can show you what to do.

Tips for Bathing and Grooming Flemish Giant Rabbits

Most rabbits shed every three months and many rabbits go through a light shed alternating with a heavier shed. Rabbits are clean animals that groom themselves, but they will need your help to keep shedding under control and to remove mats and tangles.

For Flemish Giant rabbits since they have a short coat, you only need to groom them at least once a week to keep their fur in good condition. A slicker brush is also recommended. If the rabbit is molting, usually during spring or fall season, you may have to brush him twice a week. Grooming your rabbit regularly is required because your Flemish Giant could swallow their own fur which will cause wool blocks in their intestines. With the right kind of brush, you will reduce the risk by removing excessive hairs.

Plan to brush your Flemish Giant rabbit at least once a week – this is sufficient for short-coated breeds, though it still depends on the breed, Flemish Giant rabbits who sheds regularly may need to be brushed daily or at least a few times a week. You will get a feel for how often to brush your rabbit as you see how much he sheds on a regular basis.

While brushing your Flemish Giant rabbit is highly recommended, bathing him is not. You may be surprised to learn that most rabbits hate getting wet and giving your rabbit a bath could actually be extremely stressful for him. The only time where a bath could be beneficial for your rabbit is if he has a high fever and your vet recommends a cooling bath to bring down his body temperature. It takes a rabbit a very long time to dry, so bathing could actually put your rabbit at risk for pneumonia. You are better off spot-cleaning his coat as needed with a damp cloth.

Grooming sessions is a great way for you to bond with your furry pet so make it fun for you and your pet!

Other Grooming Tasks

In addition to brushing your Flemish Giant rabbit on a regular basis, there are some other simple grooming tasks you should be prepared to perform fairly often. These include trimming your rabbit's nails, cleaning his ears, and taking care of his teeth.

Trimming Your Rabbit's Nails

When trimming your rabbit's nails you need to be very careful. Your rabbit's nails each contain a quick – that is the pink part at the base of the nail that contains the blood vessel and nerves for that nail. If your clip your rabbit's nails too short, you could sever the quick – not only will that be painful for your rabbit, but it could lead to profuse bleeding as well. When trimming your rabbit's nails, it is best to just trim off the sharp tip. Always keep some styptic powder handy to stop the bleeding in case you cut the nail too short.

Cleaning Your Rabbit's Ears

Since Flemish Giant rabbits naturally have erect ears, he may not be prone to ear infections than rabbits with low-lying ears. If your rabbit's ears get wet, they could harbor bacteria growth which could lead to an infection. Rabbits with erect ears have a lower risk for infection because their ears are open and get plenty of air flow. If you need to clean your rabbit's ears, dip a cotton ball in a mild antiseptic solution and squeeze out any excess liquid. Use the cotton ball to wipe any ear wax or debris from your rabbit's ears then let them air dry.

Caring for Your' Rabbit's Teeth

Many rabbit owners do not realize that their rabbit's teeth grow continuously. It is entirely possible for your rabbit's teeth to become overgrown which could cause him difficulty with eating. Your rabbit has four large incisors at the front of his mouth which are used to slice through vegetation – there are two upper and two lower. But there is also a pair of smaller incisors called peg teeth which are located just behind the upper incisors. Your rabbit also has eight cheek teeth further back in his mouth which is used to grind food into smaller pieces.

Your rabbit's teeth grow continuously, that's why you need to make sure he gets the right kind of food that will wear his teeth down, preventing overgrowth. If you feed your rabbit a pellet-only diet, you shouldn't be surprised if he your pet developed dental problems such as malocclusion.

Malocclusion is when the teeth don't meet properly. Making sure your rabbit gets plenty of dietary fiber is the key to keeping his teeth properly worn down. You should also have your rabbit's teeth checked by a veterinarian twice a year – he can trim your rabbit's teeth if necessary.

Chapter Eight: Showing Flemish Giant Rabbits

The Flemish Giant is a wonderful rabbit to keep as a pet but this breed has the potential to be so much more than that. In order to show your Flemish Giant rabbit, however, you have to make sure that he meets the requirements for the breed standard and you need to learn the basics about showing rabbits.

In this chapter you will learn more about the specific standard for the Flemish Giant breed and receive some tips for entering your rabbit in a show. This information will help you to decide if showing your Flemish Giant rabbit is really something you want to do.

Flemish Giant Rabbit Breed Standards

Before entering your Flemish Giant rabbit into a show, you need to make sure that he meets all of the qualifications. Judging for rabbit shows is based on the standard for each breed which is published by the governing body that is holding the show – generally the ARBA in the

United States or the BRC in the U.K. Make sure that you have a copy of the breed standard for whatever show you plan to enter and compare your rabbit to that standard.

It is important to note that if your rabbit doesn't meet the qualifications, you should not enter him in the show because you will be disqualified, so check everything first. In the next pages you'll find an overview of Flemish Giant rabbit breed standards.

Flemish Giant Rabbit (ARBA) Summary of Breed Standard:

Total Points (100)

Head – 5 points

Ears – 5 points

Body – 15 points

Size and Weight – 25 points

Legs and Feet – 10 points

Condition, Color, Flesh and Fur – 40 points

Head

- Should be large, broad and shapely
- Proportionate with the body

Ears

- Should be long, strong, thick and erect
- Must be well set on with a heavy stocky base

Body

- Must be large and powerful as possible
- Should not be flat and should have a full broad fore and hind quarters
- A full plump chest is also required
- The body should gracefully arch back from shoulders over hind legs
- Hind quarters should be as thick and massive as possible

Size and Weight

- Should be as large and powerful as possible
- Massive built but proportionate throughout

Legs and Feet

- Should be strong and straight
- Must be large and powerful
- Must be proportional to the body

Coat, Flesh and Fur Condition

- Coat should be short and glossy
- Must appear as full of life and brightness, not dead or dull
- Must be firm solid flesh
- Fur should be close and soft
- Must be free from moult

Faults

A pinched rump, paunchy, over fat, flabby, narrow body; thin ears, weak base; thin or very short coat; long or soft coat; flying coat.

Disqualifications

A short blocky body with no arch; length under 20 inches on seniors measured from end of the nose to base of the tail; ears that tip at ends, and length under 5 3/4"; short legs; fine thin bone; cow hocks; flat feet or weak ankles; toenails not matching on the same foot or corresponding foot.

Showroom Classes and Weights

- Senior bucks must be 8 months old and over, weight 13lbs or over.

- Senior does 8 months old or older, weight 14lbs or over.

Intermediate bucks and does 6-8 months of age

- Junior bucks and does under 6 months of age minimum weight for juniors is 6.5lbs

Important Note

For any changes in weight or descriptions please refer to American Rabbit Breeders Association (ARBA's) Standard of Perfection, 2006-2010 Edition, pages 123-124. You may contact the American Rabbit Breeders Association for an updated Standard of Perfection.

Flemish Giant Rabbit (BRC) Summary of Breed Standard:

Total Points (100)

- **Color** – 30 points
- **Size & Weight** – 20 points
- **Body** – 15 points
- **Legs & Feet** – 15 points
- **Head & Ears** – 10 Points
- **Coat & Condition** – 10 points

Body Type

- Should be large, roomy and flat
- Must have broad fore and hindquarters
- Does shall have a dewlap that is evenly carried

Size & Weight

- Bucks shall not be less than 4.974kg (11lb) and does not less than 5.44kg (12lb)
- Size shall be considered irrespective of weight

Head

- Should be large, full and shapely
- Dark face is allowed

Eyes

- Bold and bright
- Should be dark brown in color

Ears

- Should be erect and well set

Legs & Feet

- Shall be in length proportionate to body
- Must have strong bone
- Should be large and straight
- Feet shall be velvety, dark and ticked. Ticking to show when coat rubbed back

Coat & Condition

- Full and short coat
- Should be firm in flesh and moderately thick
- Must be free from cold

Color

- Dark steel grey, with even or wavy ticking over the whole of the body, head, ears, chest and feet alike, except belly and under tail which shall be white, upon the surface of the fur.
- Any grey, steel, sandy or other shade on the belly or under tail, except a streak of grey in each groin shall be disqualified

Amplification of Color

- The under should be blue at the base for a little more than a third of the length, then black, merging into a creamy, or bluish white ticking which may be again tipped with black.
- In even ticked specimens, the mixture should show half grey and half black tipped hairs over half of the body, neck, face and ears, but may be interspersed with longer yet - black hairs, both even and wavy ticking being permissible.
- The whole should be uniform in color
- The underparts to be white with blue undercolour
- Tail should be ticked rather darker on top, white on the underside

Important Note

For any changes in weight or descriptions please refer to British Rabbit Council Mono Breeds Standard, 2016-2020 Edition. You may contact the British Rabbit Council for updated standards.

Preparing Your Rabbit for Show

After making sure that your Flemish Giant rabbit is an excellent specimen of the breed, you can start thinking about entering a show. The first thing you need to do is become a member of whatever organization you hope to show your rabbit with – this will likely be either the ARBA or the BRC. Once you have become a member you will be able to register your rabbit under your name and enter him in shows. It can sometimes take a little while to complete this process so stay up to date with shows in your area so you can enter your rabbit as soon as your registration is completed.

When you are ready to enter your rabbit into a show, start by reading the rules and regulations for that specific show. In most cases, registering your rabbit for a show is fairly easy but you want to make sure you don't overlook anything that might get you disqualified. Make sure you adhere to the deadlines for registration and have all of the information you are likely to need handy.

Here is the information needed to compete:

- Your name and address
- The breed of your rabbit
- Your rabbit's color and age
- The sex of your rabbit
- Whether you bred or transferred the rabbit
- Whether you are a juvenile exhibitor

Once you have registered your rabbit all that is left is to wait until the show day. Prior to the day of show, make sure that you know how to get there and make sure you have a copy of the schedule so you know exactly when your rabbit is to be shown. In the days leading up to the show you should put together a kit of items that may come in handy on show day.

Keep in mind the following things needed:

- Your registration information
- Food and water for your rabbit
- Nail clippers – for emergency nail trimming
- Hydrogen peroxide – for cleaning injuries and spots on white coats
- Slicker brush and other grooming supplies

- Business cards, contact information
- Paper towels and wet wipes
- Scrap carpet square – for last-minute grooming
- Collapsible stool – when chairs are not available
- Extra clothes, food, and water for self

On the day of the show, plan to arrive at the venue at least 30 minutes prior to judging, and then proceed to your assigned pen. At this point, the best thing to do is to sit back and watch – you can learn a lot just by observing at a rabbit show. When it comes time for judging, all you can really do is wait and let the judges do their duties. Your rabbit must remain in his pen for the duration of the judging. If you rabbit wins anything, a prize card will be placed on his pen. When the judging is over, you can take your prize cards to the secretary and collect your prize money.

At this time, you can feel free to leave the show or you can stick around to keep learning. Take advantage of this opportunity to connect with other rabbit owners – you never know what you might learn or how a new connection could benefit you.

Chapter Nine: Keeping Your Rabbit Healthy

You as the owner should be aware of the potential threats and diseases that could harm the wellness of your rabbit. Just like human beings, you need to have knowledge on these diseases so that you can prevent it from happening in the first place. You will find tons of information on the most common problems that may affect your rabbit including its causes, signs and symptoms, remedies and prevention. While you may not be able to prevent your rabbit from getting sick in certain situations, you can be responsible in educating yourself about the diseases that could affect your rabbit.

The more you know about these potential health problems, the better you will be able to identify them and to seek immediate veterinary care when needed.

Common Health Problems Affecting Rabbits

Pet rabbits can be affected by a number of different health problems and they are generally not specific to any particular breed. Feeding your rabbit a nutritious diet will go a long way in securing his total health and wellbeing, but sometimes rabbits get sick anyway. If you want to make sure that your rabbit gets the treatment he needs as quickly as possible you need to learn how to identify the symptoms of disease. These symptoms are not always obvious, either – your rabbit may not show any outward signs of illness except for a subtle change in behavior.

The more time you spend with your rabbit, the more you will come to understand his behavior – this is the key to catching health problems early. At the first sign that something is wrong with your rabbit you should take inventory of his symptoms – both physical and behavioral – so you can relay them to your veterinarian who will then make a diagnosis and prescribe a course of treatment. The sooner you identify these symptoms, the sooner your vet can take action and the more likely your rabbit will be to make a full recovery.

Rabbits are prone to a wide variety of different diseases, though some are more common than others. For the benefit your rabbit's long-term health, take the time to learn the causes, symptoms, and treatment options for some of the most common health problems.

Below are some of the most common health problems that can occur to Flemish Giant rabbits. You will learn some guidelines on how these diseases can be prevented and treated as well as its signs and symptoms.

Calcivirus

Also known as viral hemorrhagic disease (VHD), rabbit calcivirus disease is a viral disease that is highly infectious, particularly among wild rabbits.

Diagnosis

This disease causes severe fever accompanied by inflammation of the intestines, damage to the lymph nodes, and even liver damage. It may be detected through medical check – up by your vet or through blood tests and other other medical examination.

If left untreated, calcivirus can lead to a condition affecting the blood which prevents it from coagulating – it can also lead to massive ruptures of blood vessels in various organs.

Signs and Symptoms

Unfortunately, most rabbits affected by calcivirus do not show any outward signs and many die within 24 hours of the onset of fever.

Some of the symptoms that your rabbit may show include difficulty breathing, weight loss, lethargy, paralysis, and convulsions. This disease is spread through direct contact or through contact with contaminated food, water or bedding.

Prevention and Treatment

To prevent the spread of virus, it is highly recommended that you always keep your rabbit's cage clean and sanitize. Unfortunately, there is no effective treatment for this disease and it is usually fatal.

Myxomatosis

In the U.S. this disease is most commonly seen along the Pacific coast, though there are different strains that occur in other parts of the country. This viral disease has also been introduced into Australia, Belgium, and other countries where it has become a major problem.

Cause

This is a viral infection known to affect rabbits and it is caused by a virus in the Poxvirus family. This disease is generally transmitted through insects and, in many cases, it is fatal. Myxomatosis is spread through blood-sucking insects like mosquitos, ticks, and lice, though direct transmission is possible.

Signs and Symptoms

Clinical signs may vary depending on the strain but may include lethargy, loss of appetite, fever, swelling around the eyes, and swelling or drooping of the ears.

Prevention and Treatment

Unfortunately, there is no effective treatment for myxomatosis and it is usually fatal. The best way to prevent this disease from occurring is to protect your rabbit against external parasites. If your rabbit does catch the disease, you need to employ careful sanitation practices to prevent spread – this virus is extremely resistant to inactivation – it takes a lot to kill the virus. Rabbits exposed to myxomatosis must be quarantined for 14 days to confirm infection.

Urine Burn

Also known as urine scald, urine burn occurs when urine soaks into the rabbit's fur and causes severe inflammation and hair loss.

Cause

This condition is common when strict sanitation practices are not followed. If you do not clean your rabbit's cage often enough or if you fail to keep his litter box fresh, your rabbit may be forced to sit in his own urine which can lead to this painful condition.

This problem can also develop from a rabbit's inability to control his bladder due to some underlying medical condition or a physical inability to assume the right stance for urination.

Signs and Symptoms

The most common sign of urine burn in rabbits is inflammation and redness around the private area.

Prevention and Treatment

The best treatment for this is to apply a soothing ointment. You should also take steps to improve the sanitation in your rabbit's cage to prevent a recurrence of the problem. The key is to keep your rabbit's cage clean and dry at all times.

Abscesses

An abscess is a pocket of fluid and pus generally cause by a bacterial infection. These are fairly common in domestic rabbits and they can form anywhere on the rabbit's body.

Cause

The cause of an abscess could be any number of things including a bite, a cut, or some other kind of wound – they may also be caused by foreign bodies becoming embedded in the rabbit's skin or mouth. They can also be the result of wounds in the mouth caused by dental disease.

Signs and Symptoms

A mouth abscess can be very painful for your Flemish Giant rabbit and it may cause him to stop eating – he may also drool and drop bits of food when he does eat. Abscesses on the skin usually appear as hard lumps.

Prevention and Treatment

The best treatment for an abscess is to drain the fluid and pus which is usually performed under general anesthesia. Following the drainage, the wound must be kept clean and the rabbit should take antibiotics to prevent infection. Painkillers may also be prescribed by veterinarian.

Coccidiosis

This disease is incredibly common in rabbits all over the world and it is caused by a protozoa, called *Eimeria* protozoa. This disease is transmitted through contaminated feed or water and, even if a rabbit recovers, he may remain a carrier of the disease and can pass it to others.

2 Types of Coccidiosis:

- **Hepatic Coccidiosis**

  Hepatic coccidiosis affects the liver and it is commonly seen in young rabbits

- **Intestinal Coccidiosis**

  This other type affects the intestines and can occur in any rabbit.

Signs and Symptoms

Rabbits with hepatic coccidiosis generally exhibit reduced appetite and poor coat condition. In most cases, the rabbit does shortly after symptoms appear. Rabbits with intestinal coccidiosis usually have a mild case with few to no symptoms which can be dangerous, certain laboratory tests may be needed to make a diagnosis.

Prevention and Treatment

Improving sanitation in the rabbit's cage is effective in eliminating hepatic coccidiosis, though it may not be as effective for intestinal coccidiosis. For proper treatment, consult your veterinarian.

E. Cuniculi

This disease is caused by a small protozoan parasite called *Encephalitozoon Cuniculi*. This parasite can be absorbed into the rabbit's body through the intestines and it generally causes lesions on the kidneys, brain, and other organs. Researchers estimate that as many as 50% of domestic rabbits carry this parasite in their bodies but only a small percentage actually develops into problems. This parasite can even be passed down from mother to baby or through direct contact with an infected rabbit.

Signs and Symptoms

The most common symptoms of E. Cuniculi include loss of balance, head tilt, tremors, convulsions, blindness, partial paralysis, and coma or death.

Prevention and Treatment

The treatment most commonly prescribed for this disease is Panacur – it can be administered in a 28-day course to destroy the parasite, though some veterinarians recommend retreatment four times a year to prevent reinfection. It is important to note, however, that this treatment is only effective in killing the parasite before symptoms appear. Plus, even if your rabbit responds to treatment he may be left with a permanent disability such as head tilt.

Pasteurellosis

Also known as "sniffles,"pasteurellosis is a common disease in rabbits. When caught early, pasteurella can be treated but, if left untreated, it can quickly become chronic or even fatal.

Cause

This disease is a respiratory infection caused by the bacteria *Pasteurella multocida* and it is highly infectious. There are several different strains of the bacteria which can affect the rabbit's eyes, ears, and various other organs.

Signs and Symptoms

The signs of pasteurella can vary depending on the strain and the progression of the disease but generally include a watery nasal discharge, sneezing, and a loud snuffling or snoring sound. This disease can also travel to the eyes, causing conjunctivitis, and to the ears, causing head shaking, head tilt, disorientation, and a loss of balance. It is also possible for this disease to affect the rabbit's reproductive tract and it may also result in the formation of abscesses (or pus-filled sores).

Prevention and Treatment

This disease is so contagious and dangerous, prevention through strict sanitation and quarantine procedures is a must.

The most common treatment for pasteurella is a 14 to 30-day course of antibiotics and supplementary probiotics.

<u>Pneumonia</u>

Pneumonia is fairly common in domestic rabbits and it is generally caused by some kind of infection – bacterial or viral in most cases – which leads to inflammation in the lungs.

Cause

Pneumonia can result from four different types of infections. It can either be bacterial, viral, fungal, or parasitic.

It is also possible for environmental factors such as chemicals, smoke, or dental disease to cause inflammation which leads to pneumonia.

Signs and Symptoms

There are four main types of pneumonia all of which exhibit similar symptoms such as anorexia, weight loss, fever, sneezing, drooling, nasal discharge, eye discharge, abscesses, and difficulty breathing.

Prevention and Treatment

The type of infection will determine the severity of the disease as well as the proper course of treatment. Rabbits suffering from fever, anorexia, weight loss, or lethargy may require fluid and electrolyte therapy. Your vet may also prescribe antiviral, antimicrobial, antifungal, or antibiotic medications depending on the type of infection causing your rabbit's pneumonia. During treatment, your rabbit's movement should be restricted.

Ringworm

Though the name might suggest otherwise, ringworm is not a disease caused by a worm or any other parasite – it is a fungal infection common in rabbits.

Causes

There are several different types of fungus which can cause ringworm in rabbits and it can actually be transmitted to humans as well. In many cases, a rabbit is infected with the fungus by another rabbit or by another household pet who is a carrier but remains asymptomatic. Poor sanitation, stress, high humidity, overcrowding, and malnutrition can all increase your Flemish Giant rabbit's risk for succumbing to this infection.

Signs and Symptoms

The first sign of ringworm in most cases is the development of patchy areas of hair loss that are dry and flaky. Rabbits generally development lesions on their head, legs and feet first which can then spread to other parts of the body.

Prevention and Treatment

Most rabbits recover from ringworm without treatment if sanitation in their cage improves. In some cases, however, treatment with anti-fungal medications may be necessary. During treatment you also need to thoroughly clean and disinfect everything in the cage to prevent reinfection.

Skin Mites

Skin mites are also sometimes called mange mites and they represent one of the most common skin problems in domestic rabbits. The most common mites to cause problems in rabbits are Cheyletiella mites which are invisible to the naked eye and can be easily spread through contaminated hay and bedding.

Causes

The cause of skin mite infestations is still unknown, but it is likely that some rabbits carry the mites unknowingly and problems only develop when the rabbit is weakened by stress, illness, or injury. Skin mites feed on keratin which leads to poor coat condition and quality.

Signs and Symptoms

The most common sign of skin mites in rabbits is patches of dandruff appearing on the coat, usually at the base of the tail and the nape of the neck. In cases of severe infection, the patch may actually look like it is moving because it is so heavily covered in mites.

Prevention and Treatment

Treatment for skin mites generally involves ivermectin injection as well as a thorough cleaning and disinfecting of the rabbit's habitat. Regular grooming will also help prevent reinfection by removing dead hairs that mites could eat.

Error! Bookmark not defined.Preventing Illness

In addition to learning about the different diseases to which your Flemish Giant rabbit may be prone, there are some other simple things you can do to keep your rabbit healthy. For one thing, you need to keep your rabbit's cage clean. Not only will cleaning your rabbit's cage help to prevent the spread of parasites, bacteria, and other harmful pathogens but it will also help to keep your rabbit's stress level low – if you rabbit becomes stressed, it could compromise his immune system and he may be more likely to get sick if he is exposed to some kind of illness.

It is important to note that you should also be mindful of making sure that your rabbit gets the right vaccinations and you should take steps to protect your Flemish Giant rabbit against parasites.

In this section you will find guidelines on how you can prevent unwanted illnesses that could endanger your rabbit's life.

- **Sanitize Your Rabbits Cage**

When it comes to cleaning your Flemish Giant rabbit's cage, there are two main goals you want to accomplish; removing debris and disinfecting everything.

Start by emptying everything out of your rabbit's cage – that includes bedding, food bowls, toys, and, of course, your rabbit. After cleaning out your rabbit's cage, disinfect it with a rabbit-friendly cleaner. Distilled white vinegar is a natural disinfectant that won't harm your rabbit or leave any residues. If you want something stronger you can mix chlorine bleach at a ratio of 1 part bleach to 5 parts water –

just be sure to thoroughly rinse everything after disinfecting it.

After cleaning and disinfecting your rabbit's cage you need to do the same for his food and water equipment as well as any toys or cage accessories. Again, you can prepare a bleach solution by mixing 1 part bleach to 5 parts water and soak everything in it before rinsing well. Make sure everything is completely dry before putting it back in the cage.

When you are done cleaning and disinfecting, add some fresh bedding to the cage and put everything back. As long as you keep to a regular schedule, you shouldn't have to clean your rabbit's cage more than once a week.

- **Preventing Parasites**

    Just like your rabbit or cat needs protection against fleas and other parasites, so do your Flemish Giant rabbit. Rabbit can attract the same kind of fleas that rabbits attract, so consider protecting your rabbit with a topical flea control preventive, it is recommended that you ask your veterinarian for recommendations on which brand to use and follow the dosing instructions very carefully.

    You should also be mindful of your rabbit's risk for mites and lice. Fur mites can cause dry, flakey patches of irritation on your rabbit's skin and ear mites can cause your rabbit's ears to become itchy and covered with wax and debris. Talk to your veterinarian if you notice any of these problems happening to your rabbit.

Recommended Vaccinations

Rabbits are not like rabbits and cats in that they need to be vaccinated against a half dozen different diseases.

There is really only one that is commonly given to rabbits – calcivirus. Your rabbit should be vaccinated for calcivirus between 10 and 12 weeks of age and then every 12 years after to maintain your rabbit's immunity.

Signs of Possible Illnesses

- **Eating Disorders** – does your rabbit show signs of appetite loss or drooling and dropping of food?
- **Coat** - does its coat and skin still feel soft, firm and rejuvenated? If your rabbit is sick sometimes, it appears physically on its body and can have a poor coat condition or hair loss.
- **Mobility** – does your rabbit looks like it is out of balance? It may be a sign of paralysis or convulsions

- **Eyes** - are there any discharge in the eyes? Is it swelling?
- **Ears** – does the ear of your rabbit swells or droops?
- **Respiratory** – does your rabbit have difficulty in breathing?
- **Nose** - does your rabbit have a watery nasal discharge? Does it snore loudly?
- **Overall Physique** - does your rabbit stays active or are there any signs of weakness and deterioration?

Rabbit Care Sheet

Congratulate yourself! You are now on your way to becoming a very well-informed and pro-active Flemish Giant rabbit owner! Finishing this book is a huge milestone for you and your future or present pet, but before this ultimate guide comes to a conclusion, keep in mind the most important things you have acquired through reading this book.

This chapter will outline the summary of what you have learned, including the checklist you need to keep in mind to ensure that you and your Flemish Giant rabbit lived happily ever after!

Basic Information

Pedigree: descendants of Patagonian rabbit; large size breed

Group: the British Rabbit Council (BRC), American Rabbit Breeders Association (ARBA), United States Flemish Giant Rabbit Club and the European Confederation of Rabbits, Pigeons and Poultry.

Breed Size: Large and Long

Length: 32 inches (80 cm)

Weight: average of 14 – 20 pounds

Coat Length: short furry coat

Coat Texture: fine, silky, smooth

Color: Black, Blue, Fawn, Light Gray, Steel Gray, Sandy, and White.

Mane: Single or Double

Temperament: docile, gentle, friendly, active

Strangers: may be wary or scared around strangers

Other Rabbits: generally good with other rabbit breeds if properly trained and socialized

Other Pets: friendly with other pets but if not properly introduce may result to potential aggression

Training: intelligent, responsive and very trainable

Exercise Needs: provide toys for mental and physical stimulation

Health Conditions: generally healthy but predisposed to common illnesses such as Urine Burn, Pasteurellosis, Pneumonia, E. Cuniculi, Ringworm, Hepatic and Intestinal Coccidiosis, Abscesses and Calcivirus

Lifespan: average 8 to 10 years

Habitat Requirements

Ideal Habitat: free-run in the home with some kind of shelter or large cage with opportunities to exercise

Cage Requirements: large enough for rabbit to move freely, easy to clean, safe

Minimum Cage Size: at least 4 to 6 times the length of the rabbit when stretched out

Ideal Cage Size: 24 x 36 x48 or an XL size similar to a dog crate with litter pan and bed

Exercise Requirements: at least everyday

Indoor vs. Outdoor: outdoor has more space, easier to clean, less noise and odor; indoor is safer, better for human interaction, and easier to monitor

Cage Accessories: water bottle, food bowl, hay rack, litter pan, nest box/shelter, toys

Recommended Bedding: meadow hay, timothy hay, natural fiber blanket

Bedding to Avoid: straw, shredded newspaper or cardboard, wood shavings, pine or cedar

Litter Training: place litter tray in the area your rabbit habitually uses to relieve himself

Recommended Litter: fresh hay lined with newspaper

Litter to Avoid: cat litter, clumping litter, scented litter, dusty litter

Nutritional Needs

Diet Type: herbivore

Nutrition Basics: low protein, high fiber

Dietary Staples: high-quality commercial pellets, grass hay, oat hay, fresh vegetables, fresh fruits

Pellets: at least 18% fiber, purchase no more than 6 weeks' worth at a time to keep fresh

Hay: alfalfa hay is okay for babies; timothy hay and other grass hays are a staple; supplement with oat hay

Vegetables: leafy greens should make up 75% of fresh diet; feed about 1 to 2 cups per 6 pounds of bodyweight daily

Fruit: no more than 1 to 2 ounces per 6 pounds of bodyweight daily

Water: unlimited access to fresh water at all times

Baby Rabbits: mother's milk until 7 weeks; start introducing alfalfa hay and pellets at 3 to 4 weeks; unlimited hay and pellets at 7 weeks; introduce veggies at 12 weeks

Young Adults: increase timothy hay, grass hay, and oat hay; decrease alfalfa hay; decrease pellets to ½ cup per 6 pounds bodyweight; increase vegetables and fruits

Mature Adults: unlimited timothy hay, grass hay, and oat hay; ¼ to ½ cup pellets per 6 pounds bodyweight; minimum 2 cups vegetables per 6 pounds bodyweight; ration no more than 2 oz. fruit per 6 pounds bodyweight daily

Senior Rabbits: maintain adult diet as long as healthy weight is stable; add alfalfa hay or increase pellet consumption for underweight rabbits

Breeding Information

Sexual Maturity (female): average 6 to 7 months old

Sexual Maturity (male): average 6 to 7 months old

Breeding Age (female): around 9 months to 1 year

Breeding Age (male): around 6 months

Breeding Type: multiple cycles per year, continuous

Mating Protocol: add the doe to the buck's cage; rebreed at least one for better chance of success

Palpation: should be able to feel marble-sized embryos after about 2 weeks since mating

Litter Size: average of 5 to 12 kits

Gestation Period: around 28 to 31 days

Nesting Box: minimum requirement is about 24 x 30 x36

Bedding: soft straw, haw, or pine shavings; mother will add some of her own fur

Characteristics at Birth: eyes and ears closed, little to no fur, completely dependent on mother

Fur Development: 5 to 6 days

Eyes Open: 10 to 12 days

Begin Weaning: around 4 weeks; does will reduce milk production after 3 weeks

Rebreeding: for continuous litters, breed again 2 to 3 weeks after kindling

Index

C

D

E

F

Q

R

S

T

U

V

W

Photo Credits

Page 1 Photo By Tjflex2 via Flickr.com, <https://www.flickr.com/photos/tjflex/9021299758/>

Page 2 Photo By Nadja Robot via Flickr.com, <https://www.flickr.com/photos/nadja_robot/8148264793/>

Page 17 Photo By Jamjar via Flickr.com, <https://www.flickr.com/photos/jamjar/10092980506/>

Page 32 Photo By Josh More via Flickr.com, <https://www.flickr.com/photos/guppiecat/9351798196/>

Page 43 Photo By Tjflex2 via Flickr.com, <https://www.flickr.com/photos/tjflex/7620096502/>

Page 51 Photo By Annie Seikonia via Flickr.com, <https://www.flickr.com/photos/21299178@N03/8036284859/>

Page 56 Photo By Houroumono via Flickr.com, <https://www.flickr.com/photos/hourou/8104684873/>

Page 64 Photo By The Original Turtle via Flickr.com, <https://www.flickr.com/photos/58638411@N00/6262667019/>

Page 65 Photo By Jamjar via Flickr.com, <https://www.flickr.com/photos/jamjar/14176682328/>

Page 71 Photo By Malcolm Payne via Flickr.com, <https://www.flickr.com/photos/malcolmp/9462852336/>

Page 79 Photo By Josh More via Flickr.com, <https://www.flickr.com/photos/guppiecat/9351796518/>

Page 80 Photo By Tjflex2 via Flickr.com, <https://www.flickr.com/photos/tjflex/9019077527/>

Page 91 Photo By Tjflex2 via Flickr.com, <https://www.flickr.com/photos/tjflex/7620148702/>

Page 110 Photo By Emilie Rhaupp via Flickr.com, <https://www.flickr.com/photos/emraps/14337136483/>

References

"7 Big Facts about the Flemish Giant" Mental Floss
<http://mentalfloss.com/article/62965/7-big-facts-about-flemish-giant-rabbit

"10 Vital Pros and Cons of Rabbits as Pets" NLCATP
<http://nlcatp.org/10-vital-pros-and-cons-of-rabbits-as-pets/>

"Breed Standard" British Rabbit Council
<http://www.thebrc.org/Mono%20Breeds%20Standards%202016-2020.pdf>

"Choosing Your Pet Rabbit" House Rabbit Resource
  Network
 <http://rabbitresource.org/care-and-health/you-and-your-rabbit/choosing-your-pet-rabbit/>

"Cleaning Rabbit Cages" Rabbit Breeders
<http://rabbitbreeders.us/cleaning-rabbit-cages>

"Disorders and Diseases of Rabbits" The Merck Manual
  Pet Health Edition
<http://www.merckvetmanual.com/pethealth/exotic_pets/rabbits/disorders_and_diseases_of_rabbits.html>

"Flemish Giants" Jany Farmer Rabbits
<http://janyfarmer-rabbits.tripod.com/flemish-giants.html>

"Flemish Giant Rabbit" LovetoKnow
<http://small-pets.lovetoknow.com/rabbits/flemish-giant-rabbit>

"Flemish Giant Rabbit History and ARBA Standard" Tiny Rabbitry
<http://tinyrabbitry.weebly.com/flemish-giant-history.html>

"Going to Shows" The British Rabbit Council
<http://www.thebrc.org/going-to-shows.htm>

"Housing" House Rabbit Society
<http://rabbit.org/faq-housing/>

"Housing and Companionship for Your Rabbits" Blue Cross for Pets
<https://www.bluecross.org.uk/pet-advice/housing-and-companionship-your-rabbits>

"Licensing and Registration under the Animal Welfare Act" APHIS
<https://www.aphis.usda.gov/animal_welfare/downloads/aw/awlicreg.pdf>

"Litter Training" House Rabbit Society
<http://rabbit.org/faq-litter-training-2/>

"Rabbit Bedding" Just Rabbits
<http://www.justrabbits. com/rabbit
bedding.html#gs.sqfNHnk>

"Rabbit Care" Essendon Veterinary Clinic.
<http://essendonvet.com.au/pet-library/rabbit-care>

"Rabbit Food" House Rabbit Society
<http://rabbit.org/faq-diet/>

"Rabbit Nutrition" Vet Secure
<https://www.vetsecure.com/animalmedcen.com/articles/29>

"Rabbit Terms Glossary" The Nature Trail
<http://www.thenaturetrail.com/showing-rabbits/terms-
glossary/>

"Suggested Vegetables and Fruits for a Rabbit Diet"
House Rabbit Society
<http://rabbit.org/suggested-vegetables-and-fruits-for-a-
rabbit-diet/>

Feeding Baby
Cynthia Cherry
978-1941070000

Axolotl
Lolly Brown
978-0989658430

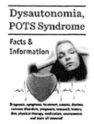

Dysautonomia, POTS
Syndrome
Frederick Earlstein
978-0989658485

Degenerative Disc
Disease Explained
Frederick Earlstein
978-0989658485

Sinusitis, Hay Fever,
Allergic Rhinitis Explained
Frederick Earlstein
978-1941070024

Wicca
Riley Star
978-1941070130

Zombie Apocalypse
Rex Cutty
978-1941070154

Capybara
Lolly Brown
978-1941070062

Eels As Pets
Lolly Brown
978-1941070167

Scabies and Lice Explained
Frederick Earlstein
978-1941070017

Saltwater Fish As Pets
Lolly Brown
978-0989658461

Torticollis Explained
Frederick Earlstein
978-1941070055

Kennel Cough
Lolly Brown
978-0989658409

Physiotherapist, Physical
Therapist
Christopher Wright
978-0989658492

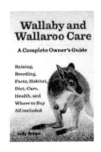

Rats, Mice, and Dormice
As Pets
Lolly Brown
978-1941070079

Wallaby and Wallaroo Care
Lolly Brown
978-1941070031

Bodybuilding Supplements
Explained
Jon Shelton
978-1941070239

Demonology
Riley Star
978-19401070314

Pigeon Racing
Lolly Brown
978-1941070307

Dwarf Hamster
Lolly Brown
978-1941070390

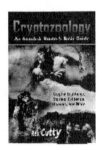

Cryptozoology
Rex Cutty
978-1941070406

Eye Strain
Frederick Earlstein
978-1941070369

Inez The Miniature Elephant
Asher Ray
978-1941070353

Vampire Apocalypse
Rex Cutty
978-1941070321

Printed in Great Britain
by Amazon